# Therese
# the Little Flower
# of Lisieux

*Written by Dorothy Smith*

*Illustrated by Robert Broomfield*

**PAULIST PRESS**
New York/New Jersey

For AMY
with love

Extracts from *Autobiography of a Saint*, Therese de Lisieux, translated by Ronald Knox, published by Fontana Books (Collins) 1958, are used by permission of the publishers.

First published in Great Britain in 1987 by McCrimmon Publishing Co Ltd, Great Wakering Essex England. Published in 1988 in the United States of America by Paulist Press, 997 Macarthur Boulevard, Mahwah, New Jersey 07430.

© 1987 Dorothy Smith

Library of Congress Cataloging-in-Publication Data

Smith, Dorothy.
    [Rainbow story of Therese, the Little Flower of Lisieux]
    Therese, the Little Flower of Lisieux/written by Dorothy
Smith: illustrated by Robert Broomfield.
    p.   cm.
    Originally published in Great Britain under title: The rainbow
story of Therese, the Little Flower of Lisieux.
    Summary: A biography of the French woman who entered the
Carmelite order at the age of fifteen, died of tuberculosis at
twenty-four, and was canonized in 1925.
    ISBN 0-8091-6577-5
    1. Therese, de Lisieux, Saint, 1873-1897—Juvenile literature. 2.
Christian saints—France—Lisieux—Biography—Juvenile litera-
ture. [1. Therese, de Lisieux, Saint, 1873-1897. 2. Saints.] I.
Broomfield, Robert, 1930- ill. II. Title.
BX4700.T5S587    1988
282'.092'4—dc19
[B]
[92]                                                            88-31651
                                                                   CIP
                                                                    AC

Cover design Robert Broomfield

Printed in Hong Kong.

# Contents

# 1. The story of a soul

ONCE, three sisters sat talking quietly together in the little town of Lisieux in Normandy, in France. They were talking about the days when they were children, and remembering their parents. The youngest of them, Therese, seemed to remember everything as vividly as if it were only yesterday. Her sisters were delighted by her stories, and Marie, the eldest, said: 'What a pity all this isn't written down for us. If you asked Therese to make a book out of her childhood memories, it would give us such pleasure!'

Therese thought her sisters were teasing her, and she laughed. But Pauline said: 'Therese, you are to write down all the memories of your childhood!'

For Marie, Pauline and Therese were not only sisters in real life; they were also sisters in the order of Carmelites, and they all lived in the Carmel Convent of Lisieux. Pauline was the Mother Prioress. Like all the other Sisters, when Therese had entered the order she had promised to obey her superiors in every detail. So when Pauline, the Mother Prioress, ordered her to begin writing down her childhood memories, she took up her pen, and for the rest of her short life she was busy writing.

She wrote directly to Pauline, who was Mother Prioress now, and whom she had called 'Little Mother' when she was a little girl at home.

'Dearest Mother,' she wrote, 'it is to you, who are my mother twice over, that I am going to tell the story of my soul. When you first asked me to do it I was frightened: it looked as if it would mean wasting my spiritual energies on introspection. But since then Our Lord has made it clear to me that all he wanted of me was plain obedience. And in any case, what I shall be doing is only what will be my task in eternity—telling over and over again the story of God's mercies to me.'

She called the book she wrote *Story of a Soul*. Other people have called it 'The Autobiography of a Saint'. The book is the reason why we know so much about this girl, who apparently did so little, and died so young, but who is loved and honoured as St Therese, the Little Flower of Lisieux.

### The Family Baby

Yet she was not born at Lisieux, but in a town about fifty miles away, called Alencon. It is a very pleasant ancient town with old houses and narrow streets. It is famous for two things—a splendid church called Notre Dame, and lovely lace called Point d'Alencon, made by the clever hands of the local women. The church and the lace were both to be important in Therese's life.

Her mother, Zelie, was an expert lace-maker herself. She ran a lace business from their home, employing other women who worked in their own homes: Zelie bought and sold their work.

Therese's father, Louis Martin, was a jeweller and clockmaker. So the Martin family were comfortably off, in a quiet way.

They lived at Number 50 Rue St Blaise in Alencon. The house is still there. It is open to visitors, who can see all the mementoes of the Martin family life, and the rooms Therese lived in when she was a very little girl.

Louis and Zelie Martin were both deeply religious. They had chosen their house because it was close to the church of Notre Dame, and they began each day by attending the early Mass at 5.30 in the morning.

They longed to have a son who would become a priest. Perhaps he might even be a missionary priest, to take the faith to lands France ruled, thousands of miles away beyond the seas. Yet this high hope was doomed to disappointment. They had two little boys, but they died as babies; and so too did two little girls.

Four daughters lived. They were growing up when Zelie was to have another baby. She was 42 years old now, and Louis was 50, so they felt that this was their last chance. They redoubled their prayers for their 'little priest'—but it was not to be.

When the baby was born, on January the 2nd 1873, it was a girl. Her parents received her as a gift from God, and she was welcomed lovingly into the family.

When so many babies died young, it was the custom to hold the christening very soon. So only two days later the baptism was held at the Church of Notre Dame. Her father was there, and her four sisters clustered round her, admiring this tiny baby in the beautiful Point d'Alencon christening robe. Marie, who was 13, Pauline, at eleven, and Leonie

and Celine, who were six and four, were ready to mother the family baby.

She was baptised Marie Francoise Therese; and so Therese Martin became a member of the Holy Catholic Church.

Years later, when she was working on her book, she wrote: 'God has seen fit to surround me with love at every moment of my life; all my earliest impressions are of smiles and endearments. And, if He planted love all about me, he planted it in my childish heart, too.'

As soon as she could walk, Therese would follow her mother about the house. As she climbed the stairs, she stopped on each step to call 'Maman, Maman!' and waited for her mother to call back to her before she went on.

Her mother and father centred their lives, and their entire family life, around their church-going. Therese was brought up to look on going to church as a privilege, even a treat.

Once, when she was three years old, she went missing. There was a frantic search for everyone's darling—and at last she was found, all alone, saying her prayers in the church.

Prayer was as natural to her as breathing, and God was as real to her as any member of her family. She was a very literal little girl, and she kept this quality all her life. She was told to love God and one day she would go to Heaven, and she believed this all her life.

Her mother laughed at her a little, when she was writing about her. 'Baby is such a quaint little creature; she comes up and puts her arms round me and wishes I were dead. When you scold her, she explains: "It's only because I want you to go to Heaven; you told me yourself nobody can go to

Heaven without dying!" She wants to kill off her father, too, when she gets really affectionate!'

Her father, who was old enough to be her grandfather, adored his youngest daughter. He called her his Little Queen, and she thought her father was the most wonderful man in the world.

Twenty years later, in a very different place, she could recapture vividly little scenes from the days when she was only a baby. By then she could see how those incidents had shaped her life.

'How quickly those sunny days of childhood pass! And yet, how those delightful memories have stamped themselves on my soul. I remember the thrill of going for a walk with Papa. The smallest details of them have left their impress on my mind, especially the Sunday walks, when Maman went with us.'

She believed the whole world was hers.

'One day Leonie, thinking she was too old to play with dolls any more, came along to Celine and me with a basket full of dresses and bits of stuff. "Here you are, darlings," she said. "Choose which you would like—they're all for you!" Celine put her hand in and brought out a little ball of silken braid which had taken her fancy. I thought for a minute, and then I held out my hand and said: "I choose everything!" Then straight away I took over the whole basket.'

'Just childishness? Perhaps. But in a sense it's been the key to my whole life. Later on, when the idea of religious perfection came to me, I found myself crying out, just as I did when I was a baby: "My God I choose everything! No point in becoming a saint by halves. I want the whole lot, everything whatsoever that is Your will for me!"'

While Therese was still very young, this happy

home was broken up. Madame Martin became very ill. There was no hope of a cure, and before Therese was five, her mother died. There was a dreadful day when her father said to her: 'Come, kiss your mother for the last time!'

It was a terrible shock for her, and the happy, carefree little girl changed completely. Now she was shy and timid, ill at ease except with her own family; ready to burst into tears at the slightest thing.

The first stage of her life ended when her mother died.

# 2. Therese at Lisieux

MONSIEUR MARTIN was now left a widower, with five daughters growing up. He was utterly bewildered by the new situation. Zelie's brother and his wife suggested he should move to Lisieux, where they lived, so that they could be at hand to help, and share his responsibilities.

So on an autumn day in 1877, little Therese arrived in Lisieux with the rest of the Martin family, rattling over the cobbles in the Place St Pierre in the station cab. 'I can't remember that I minded leaving Alencon; children enjoy a change, and I welcomed our arrival at Lisieux.'

Soon they moved into their own home. It was called Les Buissonnets—The Shrubberies—and it lay just on the outskirts of the town. The house was typical of the French middle classes a hundred years ago, solidly and comfortably furnished. It is still there to be visited, like the only other home Therese ever lived in, at Alencon. Everywhere there are pictures and statues, symbols of the religion that was the breath of life to the family. You can still see Therese's room, and her toys have been preserved so visitors can see the toys a saint played with.

Later on she had a deep understanding of life, but her experience was not very wide; so she kept referring back to these familiar surroundings, even to her toys, to try to explain her meaning.

Soon they settled down, and a quiet, happy family life built up in the new home.

'It was at Les Buissonnets that I really found life enjoyable.'

Yet there was a change: their mother was no longer there. Therese believed, as they all did, that she was safe in Heaven, and that her babyish wish had come true in a way she never expected. Yet family life could never be perfect without her—so Therese believed true happiness, for herself and her father and sisters, would be found only when they rejoined their mother in Heaven.

When Madame Martin died, Therese heard a servant pitying her for having no mother now. She flung herself on Pauline. 'Pauline will be my little Mother,' she cried. Pauline was very good to her, and tried hard to take their mother's place. She looked after Therese and taught her lessons, which had to be finished before she was allowed her favourite treat, a walk with her father.

Every day M Martin used to go for a walk in Lisieux, or in the country close by, and Therese loved to go with him. On the way back they always went into one of the churches in Lisiuex to pray before the Blessed Sacrament. One of these visits was to have great consequences.

'Every afternoon I used to go for a walk with Papa, and we made our visit to the Blessed Sacrament together. We used to go round all the churches in turn, and that's how I had my first experience of going into the chapel at Carmel. There,

Papa showed me the grille that shuts off the choir, and told me that there were nuns beyond it. The suspicion never crossed my mind that nine years later I should be one of them.'

One winter afternoon it was dark as they made their way home, and the stars were coming out. Therese could see Orion in the sky; she had just begun to learn her letters.

'Look, Papa! Look!' she exclaimed. 'There is a T in the sky! It must be for Therese. My name is written in Heaven!'

Sometimes they went on longer expeditions. M Martin loved fishing, and he used to take Therese with him all day into the peaceful Normandy countryside where streams flowed between orchards of apple trees.

As her father settled down on the bank to fish, Therese would sit silently beside him. Years later, she remembered the child she had been.

'It was a great day when he took me with him; I did so love the countryside, with all the birds and the flowers. I even tried fishing too, with a small rod of my own, but I preferred sitting there on the grass with the flowers for my company. My thoughts went deep at such times, and although I knew nothing about meditating, my soul did sink into a state of genuine prayer.'

The wistful little girl, always too ready to burst into tears, was still able to be happy at home. Her sister Celine, next in age, was her greatest friend, and they played together in the garden. Even then, their favourite games were to do with the church and its festivals. They gathered flowers to decorate home-made altars, and they built little pretend Christmas cribs in the corners of the garden.

'When one of these was finished, I ran off to fetch Papa and dragged him to the spot, making him keep

his eyes shut till he was told to open them. Obediently he would follow me to my little garden, and when I shouted "Open your eyes, Papa!" he would humour me by going into ecstacies of admiration at what seemed to me a masterpiece.'

It was not like the carefree days in Alencon; yet she was still a child. Over the next few years a series of events, all of which remained perfectly clear in her mind, were to draw her from childhood to an adult acceptance of life and her responsibilities. The first of them must have been deeply frightening; no wonder it remained as clear to her as a nightmare.

'Papa had been away for several days, and wasn't expected back for two days more. It must have been about two or three in the afternoon; the sun was shining brightly. I was standing all alone at an attic window which gave on to the main garden. Suddenly I saw, in front of the laundry just opposite, a man dressed exactly like Papa, of his own height, and walking just as he did, only much more bent as he walked. His face I couldn't see, because his head was muffled in an apron of some indeterminate colour. He wore the kind of hat that Papa usually wore. I saw him move steadily onwards, and all at once I was overcome by the sense of something uncanny about him. Then it occurred to me that Papa must have come home early, and was going about in disguise to give me a start, so I shouted, in a voice shrill with alarm: "Father! Father"

'There was no sign that the mysterious visitor had heard me; he went steadily without turning round, and I watched him making for the clump of trees which cut the main walk in two. I waited to see him come out on the farther side of those spreading branches. But no, the warning apparition had vanished.'

She told Marie and Pauline about it. They tried to calm her, and told her to think no more about it—impossible advice for something that had made such a strong impression on her.

'Constantly I tried to tear the veil from the mysterious scene I had witnessed, but it was not until 14 years later that God tore the veils aside.'

And indeed after she was in Carmel M Martin became paralysed and mentally ill. He used to try to hide his twitching face with any piece of cloth he could find. Perhaps this strange glimpse of her father as an old man was Therese's first realisation that her sheltered home life would not last for ever.

Her next experience of growing up was much more usual: she was sent to school. Like many children from a happy home, she found it a harsh shock. She had learnt her lessons from Pauline, and she was well advanced for her age, but she had no experience of being one girl in a class of others, and she was alarmed at the hurly burly of the playground.

She went as a day girl, when she was eight, to the Abbaye Des Benedictines, a big convent school on the other side of the town. Shyness and timidity still troubled her outside the family, and she was homesick and lonely during the long days at school.

'I did not like games, especially boisterous games; and not knowing how to play like other children, I did not feel I was an agreeable companion. I did my best to imitate the others, but without ever succeeding.'

She used to read, by herself, and sometimes she gave little funerals to the bodies of birds she found dead under the trees in the playground.

The days at school were long, and she looked forward all day to going home to the warmth and comfort of Les Buissonnets, and especially to Pauline's loving welcome. Since their mother had died, Therese had called Pauline Little Mother; their Father called her Lovely Pearl.

Then one day Therese was shattered by overhearing a conversation between Pauline and Marie.

Pauline said: 'I have just seen the Prioress of Carmel, and I shall probably enter next week.'

Therese gave a great cry: 'Pauline—don't go without me! Wait for me!'

She had always known that one day her sister would go away to become a nun, but she thought it would not be for a long time, when she herself was grown up. She believed that she too would become a nun, and she had hoped the two real-life sisters would enter Carmel together.

Pauline explained gently that she was called to enter the Convent of Carmel, where the nuns passed their lives in prayer. She was 20 years old now: if this was to be her life, she should not delay, even for the sake of a much loved little sister. She hoped it might be that Therese would join her there later.

Therese was impatient. She wanted to go now with Pauline. She was so insistent that Pauline took her to see the Mother Prioress of Carmel, Mother Marie de Gonzague. She told Therese she could see that she had a sincere desire to enter Carmel, but at nine years she was much too young. She must wait until she was sixteen, and then it might be possible for her to enter Carmel as a postulant, a beginner.

One of the other nuns who met Therese was very taken by her fair curly hair and blue eyes. 'How pretty she is!' she exclaimed. 'What a sweet little girl!'

Therese was upset. She wanted to be taken seriously, not just treated as a little doll. She began to think more deeply about why she really wanted to enter Carmel.

'I told Almighty God not once but many times that it was for His sake and His sake only I wanted to be a Carmelite!'

First of all she had to live through the parting from Pauline.

Therese was inconsolable. She knew Pauline would never come home again. She was no longer there to welcome her when she got back from school, and though Marie tried hard to take her place, she missed her Little Mother dreadfully.

Even the visits to Carmel were no comfort. Pauline was Sister Agnes de Jesus now, dressed in the black habit of the Carmelites, and in the parlour a grille separated her from her family, to show she had withdrawn from the world.

Therese often left these brief, painful meetings in tears. The shock of losing Pauline, and the powerful drive of her own wish to enter Carmel, made her ill. She suffered some kind of nervous illness, with delirium, violent tremblings, desperate headaches. Her sisters were really afraid she would die. They gathered beside her bedside and knelt down in front of the statue of Our Lady which stood there, and prayed for her recovery. Therese, unable to speak, and hardly able to recognise her sisters, gazed at the statue from her bed.

Suddenly she had a strange experience. The statue appeared radiantly beautiful, as if Our Lady was smiling down at her, and her alone. She no longer felt distressed and miserable, but filled with quiet happiness. She smiled at her sisters, and they knew she was going to get better.

Therese felt that moment was particularly important. She was no longer ill, but well and strong; no
longer torn apart by the loss of Pauline, but serene
and confident that one day she would join her.
Now the brief visits that were permitted were happy
times for both of them.

The next great happening of these years was to be
a source of strength, and another milestone towards
growing up. Therese was prepared for her first communion. She was aware of it then and for ever as
one of the great days of her life.

When Celine had made her first communion,
Therese had entered into all her feelings very deeply; she made every effort to learn from the instruc-
tion and prayer she received herself.

She could always recapture every detail of the day

itself—May the 8th, 1884. She was eleven years old.

'At last the day came, the greatest of all days for me; even the tiniest details of that visit to Heaven have left their imprint on my memory. The big room, and the dresses laid out there, white as snowflakes, which we put on, one after another. Then the chapel, and the lovely hymn chanted in the fresh morning air.

'But I don't want to go into details; there are scents which you can't expose to the air without their losing their fragrance, and there are experiences of the soul which you can't express in human language without losing their heavenly meaning. What comfort it brought to me, that first kiss Our Lord imprinted on my soul! A lover's kiss! There were no longer two of us—Therese had simply disappeared, like a drop lost in the ocean: Jesus only was left, My Master, My King!'

A first communion was always a great family festival, and everyone made it a happy day for her. Her father and sisters, her aunt and uncle and cousins who were part of their life in Lisieux came to Mass with her, and in the afternoon she was able to go and see Pauline.

In the evening there was a family party, and her father gave her a pretty little watch in honour of the day.

Once she was seen with tears on her cheeks, and her family wondered if she was sad because her mother, and Pauline, her 'little mother', were not there. But this time they were tears of happiness.

As she lay in bed that night, Therese lived through every moment of the day, and repeated to herself her resolve: Saviour, with love I consecrate myself to thee!'

# 3. *The Sisters of Carmel*

W HEN PAULINE left Les Buissonnets to enter
the Carmel in Lisieux, Therese knew,
although it was only two miles away, that
she would never return home, and nothing would
ever be the same again.

The Sisters who enter the Carmelite order put the
world behind them forever. They say goodbye to
family and friends; in future they may receive a
family visit once a month, in the convent parlour,
divided from them by a grille that shows how they
are separated from the world. They cannot touch
one another or exchange kisses.

The Sisters meet together in choir for the services
that break up the day, which are called the Divine
Offices. Members of the public may join them in
this church; but here, too, the community, as the
Sisters are called, are far from them, behind a grille.

This was the scene that had so impressed Therese
when her father took her into the church at Carmel
when she was a little girl.

The Sisters leave the world in order to pray for it.
They are not a nursing or a teaching order; they do
not seek to look after the old or the poor. They be-

lieve that all their lives should be spent in meditation and prayer. They spend each day of their lives in a strict pattern of prayer with the community, and in solitary prayer in their own cells.

To underline what they are trying to do, each nun takes a threefold vow. She promises to accept poverty, to be free from all worldly possessions; chastity, to be free from human affection; and obedience to the Rule of the Carmelite order, which sets the pattern of their lives.

So that they can concentrate entirely on God, they never leave their convent, and never go out again into the world they have left. A Sister spends all her life in the Carmel she first enters, unless she is sent to help form a new Carmel elsewhere.

They are enclosed in their convent, which no outsider may enter.

The convent itself is plain and bare, and cold. The Sisters eat only the plainest food, and apart from the services and the business of the community, conversation is limited to a brief daily recreation hour.

A woman drawn to this austere, dedicated life is examined carefully by the mother prioress of the order, and the convent chaplain. If they approve, she enters as a postulant for a period of some months, rather like a probationer nurse. Then she offers herself to God, as a bride of Christ. She declares she will give up earthly husband and children for his sake. She is clothed in the habit of the order, and wears the white veil of a novice. She sets aside her family name and takes a new name, 'in religion'. After another lengthy trial she takes her final vows, which are as solemn and binding as marriage vows, and she takes the black veil of the fully professed Carmelite.

It was to embrace this life that twenty-year-old Pauline Martin left home, to become Sister Agnes of Jesus in the Carmelite order.

And her sister Therese, at nine years old, longed with all her soul to follow her. This longing filled her heart for the next five years.

# 4. The road to Carmel

WHEN THERESE was thirteen, she left school with few regrets, but carried on her education through private lessons with a governess. For her, and for any other middle class French girl at that time, there was no question of being trained for a job, or going out to work. Most girls stayed quietly at home like young ladies until they were married.

Therese was still young enough to enjoy treats and presents. She enjoyed a holiday by the seaside with Celine, with donkey rides and shrimping, and she was pleased when her aunt gave her blue ribbons to tie up her fair hair. But she did not want to stay a child for ever.

There was a painful parting when Marie left home to join Pauline in Carmel, but this was not the anguished affair Pauline's departure had been. There was a real sense that the parting was not for ever. Leonie was in another convent.

Therese tried to see God's purpose for her life, looking for the day when her childish dreams could become her adult purpose. Later on she always said she knew the very minute when she grew up: it happened on a particular occasion, and at an actual moment in time. It happened very early on Christmas morning in 1886, in the sitting room of the family home.

Every Christmas, all the five little Martin girls had hurried back from midnight Mass to the hearth where they had set out their shoes, waiting to find

them packed with 'surprises'—which is what French children have instead of a Christmas stocking. Now Marie, Pauline and Leonie had left home, and Celine was a young lady of eighteen. Therese, almost fourteen was still the spoiled darling of the family, and still expected all the treats and surprises.

Back from midnight Mass, she ran upstairs to take off her hat. As she hurried downstairs, she heard her father in the sitting room, muttering: 'Surprises like this are a bit childish for a big girl like Therese. I hope this is the last year for them.'

Celine, who was just beside her, caught her arm. She knew such words could make her abnormally sensitive sister cry for hours. 'Don't go in just yet!' she murmured. 'If you do, you will only cry and upset Papa. Wait a bit!'

In that shocked moment, Therese saw her way clear before her. In the first place she didn't cry, but ran in smiling happily and opened her surprises, exclaiming in delight. She was not going to cry and make a scene and spoil the family Christmas.

In a flash, she saw she was a 'big girl' now. She must grow up, stop silly crying and childishness, stop being the family baby, stand on her own feet.

'Yes, it was on December 25th, 1886, that I was given the grace to leave my childhood's days behind. "Little Therese" had recovered her strength of mind, and recovered it for good.'

Two great ideas flowed into her mind from that moment. First of all, if she was to be a grown-up—which meant to love and serve God in a grown-up way—she must start at once. If she really saw her path leading her to Carmel, she must take it as soon as possible. That was clear to her immediately.

The second and most important idea took a while

to clarify. Indeed, she was working it out for the rest of her life, and it is the reason why she was declared a saint.

For the love of God, and of her family, she had deliberately subdued her own feelings and acted generously and kindly; and no one ever knew how difficult it had been. It was an heroic act of renunciation, and it had happened in the family sitting room. No one needs, she said later, anything else.

She had dreamed of sacrifice on a grand scale: to become a martyr; to be a second Joan of Arc. There was no need. Great deeds are unnecessary.

There is a Little Way, for ordinary people, made up of little deeds, that leads to perfection and will carry all seeking souls towards God.

The little girl in Normandy a hundred years ago probably never heard the words of the English poet, but she echoed his words in her heart:

*The daily round, the common task*
*Will furnish all we need to ask—*
*Room to deny ourselves, a road*
*To bring us daily nearer God.*

'God had to perform a miracle on a small scale to make me grow up, grow up in a moment.'

She always remembered her little miracle: she called it her Christmas Grace.

She felt she had suddenly grown up; but perhaps she was not quite grown up yet, for she wanted a positive proof that she was right. If she was to devote herself to prayer all her life, she wanted to know her prayers would be answered. 'Just for once,' she prayed, 'give me a proof.'

She received it in the strangest way. She was a

totally unworldly girl, living in a sheltered home; she was not even allowed to read the newspapers because she might read painful or evil things in them. Yet she listened to grown-up conversation, and she came to hear her father and her uncle and aunt talking about a sensational murder case that had shocked all France.

A criminal named Pranzini had murdered two women and a child in the course of a robbery. He had been arrested and condemned to death. Therese was horrified to think that if such a man died unrepentant he would be completely destroyed.

She felt it was her duty to save him from hell, and she prayed fervently not for his release but for his repentance. Of course she never set eyes on him, and he had no idea that in Lisieux an unknown girl was praying for him daily—hourly. She was praying for something else, as well.

She was certain God did mean to pardon Pranzini, but as a kind of encouragement to her to carry on praying for sinners, she asked for an actual sign that he had repented.

In spite of the rule about not reading the newspapers, she managed to follow up the Pranzini story. The day after his execution, she lost no time in opening the paper.

At the last moment, as he approached the scaffold, Pranzini had seized the crucifix in the hand of the priest attending him and kissed it! Therese was deeply stirred, and deeply grateful. This man, the child of her prayers, had met death with the crucifix pressed to his lips. Now she knew her prayers could save souls. She needed no more signs but she longed to be free to carry out this, her special work in the world.

For the next few months she was the joy of the

family as never before. She tried to think less of herself and her feelings, more of other people. She offered help with the housework to the maid of all work. Her sisters had all done their share, but baby Therese had never even had to make her own bed. She found useful work she could do with the poor children of Lisieux.

Sometimes she allowed herself to dream of the future. She knew that when she entered Carmel she would be given a new name 'in religion', and she wondered what it would be. She was very fond of her own name—it was her name in the family, and the name of the greatest of all Carmelites, Teresa d'Avila. Pauline, Sister Agnes, had 'of Jesus' after her name; but that sounded rather remote. She thought 'Therese of the Child Jesus' would be a lovely name.

She decided she would try to enter Carmel the next year, when she would be fifteen. There were many obstacles in her way, but she was filled with a firm resolve and she set out to overcome them one by one.

First of all, she had to tell her father, and get his permission.

It was hard even to ask for it: she knew how much he loved his 'little queen'. If she left home it would take the sunshine from his life.

She chose Whitsunday, when he came home from Vespers, on an evening in early summer. He sat on a bench in the garden, and she went and sat beside him. She could not speak, and her eyes were wet with tears.

'What's the matter, Little Queen?' her father asked. 'Tell me about it.'

So she told him about her longing to enter Carmel, not in the distant future, but next year when she would be fifteen. He had long realised that one day she would join Pauline and Marie; he only urged that she was still very young to make such a serious resolution.

Therese found words to explain her strength of purpose, and at last he was ready to see the will of God in her intention.

There were some little white flowers, rather like lilies, growing on a low wall close by. M Martin picked one and gave it to Therese. She noticed he had pulled up its roots, as well. She took this to mean that she, like a plant, was to take fresh life in new soil, richer than the soft moss in which it had first wakened, just as he gave her leave to find a new home on Mount Carmel.

With her father's permission secured, Therese thought it would all be plain sailing. But she had to follow the road to Carmel with one difficult step after another.

First of all, the family. Her uncle and aunt, Monsieur and Madame Guerin, had been very kind to her and had played a big part in her upbringing since the Martin family's move to Lisieux. M Guerin would have been her guardian if M Martin had died. Their approval must be sought next.

They were deeply shocked at the very idea. Her uncle, particularly, was appalled. 'It would be an unheard-of thing! It would be a scandal throughout France! The very idea of a fifteen-year-old child being allowed to enter a Carmelite convent! I shall oppose it by every means in my power!'

Therese begged him to think it over and change his mind. 'I assure you it would take a miracle to make me change my mind!' he thundered.

Therese fled before the storm and did not go back for several days. Her uncle spoke to her quietly.

'I have been thinking over what you told me, and I have been praying about it,' he said. 'Go in peace, my child. I shall not stand in your way!'

The next step was to apply to the prioress at Carmel. Mother Marie de Gonzague was delighted to see once more the little girl who had been to see her five years before, and she was ready to take her at once. But the convent chaplain, who had the final decision, thought very differently. He got angrier and angrier whenever the subject was put to him.

'Why do you keep on plaguing me about this young girl?' he demanded. 'Anyone would think the salvation of the community depended on her. Let her stay at home until she is twenty-one! I forbid you to speak to me about it again!'

This time the opposition was not melted by prayer; but at last he passed the matter on to a higher authority. 'I am only the Bishop's representative in Lisieux,' he said. 'The real decision rests with him.'

So her father escorted her to the Bishop's palace in Bayeux. She wore her smartest clothes, to look more grown up; and to make herself older, she 'put her hair up', which in those days was a milestone in the life of a young lady who had put childhood behind her.

She looked at herself in the mirror before they set out, and murmured: 'If the Bishop *won't* let me enter Carmel when I'm fifteen, I'll go to the Holy Father himself.'

The Bishop received her kindly, but almost teasingly. He asked her to sit down, and when she hesitated because his chaplain was standing, he smiled. 'There now, sit down. Don't you want to show us you know the meaning of obedience?'

But as he began to question her, he was struck by the steely resolve of his fourteen-year-old visitor. He began by asking if she had thought of being a Carmelite for a long time.

'Oh, yes, my Lord Bishop,' she replied. 'A long, long time!'

'Oh, come, it's not as long as fifteen years!'

Therese smiled back at him. 'That's true. But it is not much less than that. I've wanted to be a nun ever since I can remember, and I've set my heart on Carmel ever since I got to know it well. I've always known it was the place where my soul's longings would be set at rest.'

The Bishop looked at her rather uneasily, and asked a few more questions. He promised to consider the matter, and let her have his answer in writing. He asked what she would do in the meantime. When M Martin told him he was going to take Therese and Celine on a visit to Rome, he approved heartily.

Therese had hoped the Bishop would give his answer immediately. When he only promised to think it over, she was bitterly disappointed in the delay, which seemed a delay in fulfilling God's plan for her life. But she went along quietly with all the plans for their journey, and secretly she herself began to make a plan.

They travelled through Italy with a party of pilgrims from Lisieux, combining sightseeing with visits to the Holy Places. Therese was impressed by the splendid churches, and was thrilled by the tales of the saints and martyrs of the early Church.

They were led by their own chaplain, who had sent Therese to the Bishop, and who greatly disapproved of Therese.

The highspot of the pilgrimage was a private audience with the Pope, Leo XIII. On Sunday, November the 20th, Therese put on her ceremonial dress, black, with a lace mantilla, and a papal medal on a blue and white ribbon. As she took her place in line with the other pilgrims, the chaplain said in a harsh voice: 'It is strictly forbidden for the pilgrims to speak to the Holy Father.' And he looked suspiciously at Therese.

The Pope sat in a big armchair, wearing a white cassock and cape. One by one, each pilgrim knelt before him and received his blessing. Then the papal guard touched the pilgrim lightly on the shoulder and he got up and made way for the next.

The moment came when Therese found herself
kneeling at the feet of the Pope. He held out his
hand for her to kiss his ring, but she clasped her
hands together and began to speak.

'Most Holy Father,' she murmured, 'I have a
great favour to ask of you. In honour of your jubilee
I want you to let me enter the Carmelite order when
I am fifteen.'

The Pope turned to the chaplain, saying: 'I don't quite understand!'

The chaplain replied, loudly and unsympathetically. 'Holy Father, this *child* here is anxious to enter Carmel at fifteen, and her superiors are looking into the matter at this very moment!'

The Pope looked down kindly at the figure kneeling at his feet. 'Very well, my child. Do what your superiors tell you!'

Therese made one more effort. She put her hands on his knee and pleaded: 'Oh, most Holy Father, if only *you* would say Yes, everybody would have to agree!'

The Pope looked at her intently and said softly: 'All's well—all's well. If God wants you to enter, you will!'

The guards came forward and moved her away, while the Pope raised his hand in blessing.

The rest of their travels meant nothing to Therese. Now she was sure that when she got home she would find a letter of permission from the Bishop at Bayeux. It was not there; and Christmas came and went.

Then, on New Year's Day, 1888, she received a message from the Prioress at Carmel. The Bishop had written to say that if she thought fit, he was prepared to give his consent to Therese Martin's immediate entry into Carmel.

The next day was her fifteenth birthday.

# 5. A testing time

THE MOTHER Prioress thought it would be better if she did not start her life in Carmel with Lent—when the nuns fasted very strictly—ahead of her. She suggested that Therese should come after Easter. It was sensible advice, but Therese felt it was another obstacle in her path. The days passed slowly for her.

'Happy imprisonment—how I long for it!' she mused.

At last the time came, with the biggest obstacle of all—saying goodbye to her family and her home. Her aunt and uncle came to spend the last evening with her, along with her father and Celine.

'How harrowing they are, these farewell gatherings between close friends! Just when you'd like to fade out and be forgotten, there's a whole wealth of loving words and tender embraces which remind you of the sacrifice such a parting involves!'

It was a quiet family evening. Therese wore a pretty dress, and had her fair hair uncovered for the last time.

The next morning she said goodbye to the house and gardens of Les Buissonnets, where she had been happy, then took her father's arm and walked the short distance to Carmel, knowing she would never retrace her steps.

The rest of the family gathered in the chapel; then Therese was beckoned to the convent entrance. She kissed everyone goodbye, and her father gave her his blessing. Then she slipped through the door, into Carmel itself.

She was greeted by the whole community, including her own sisters, Marie and Pauline, who were now Sister Marie of the Sacred Heart and Sister Agnes of Jesus.

'Soon I was being embraced by Marie and Pauline, those dear sisters who had been mothers to me for so long.'

Now she was a postulant, learning to be a nun, and seeing if her strength of purpose was equal to the task that lay ahead. She dressed in a plain dark dress, with a long narrow skirt, with a little bonnet on her head, and a short cape round her shoulders. She was shown all round the convent, with its bare corridors and stairs, and the refectory, and the bare cell where she would spend many hours alone in prayer. She immediately felt at home there.

'Everything delighted me. I felt cut off from the world. Above all, how I loved my little cell. There was nothing disturbing about this delight; it was quite calm, as if the breeze was too light to rock my little boat on the water's surface, the sky too bright for a single cloud.

'All the difficult time I'd been through had been worth it after all. I could go about saying to myself, I'm here for good now, here for good!'

Why was she there? She re-stated her motive to herself as she looked round her new home, so bleak

and different from the comfortable Les Buissonnets.

'I declared in the presence of the Sacred Heart
that I'd come to Carmel to save souls, and above all
to pray for priests. Well, if you want to attain any
object, no matter what it is, you've got to find the
right steps to it. And Our Lord let me see clearly
that if I wanted to save souls I'd got to do it by
bearing a cross, so the more suffering came my way,
the more strongly did suffering attract me.'

Her suffering began the very moment she
embraced her sisters. The convent chaplain, who
had so much opposed her, remarked cuttingly:
'Sing a Te Deum, Reverend Mother, if you can. As
the Bishop's representative, I present you with this
fifteen-year old child. I hope she will not fail to
come up to your expectations. If not, remember you
have only yourselves to thank. I have taken no responsibility for her.'

Even this singularly ungracious, indeed unchris-
tian, welcome did not daunt Therese. She was aware
of the problems ahead, and she tried to face them.

She might cling to Marie and Pauline, her real
sisters, so much that people might think she had
entered Carmel just to be with them. From the very
first, Therese disciplined herself never to seek them
out, not to talk with them in the brief recreation
hour, so that they might never seem to mean more
to her than her new sisters in God.

The other risk was that the little girl might become a convent pet, indulged by everyone as she
had been when she was a child at home. Yet it was
to avoid that, that she had left home, to be taken
seriously.

The Prioress, Mother Marie de Gonzague, was
also determined to prevent that happening. She fol-

lowed a policy of picking on Therese and humiliating her. Perhaps she thought it would be good for her, or perhaps she was jealous of the group of the three Martin sisters in the convent. Anyway, if Therese was looking for suffering in daily life, Mother Marie de Gonzague made sure she found it.

Postulants do all the housework in Carmel, and Therese had hardly ever done any at home. The Prioress would say: 'It's easy to see that our convent is being swept by a fifteen-year-old girl! Look at those cobwebs! What a pity!'

Or she would meet Therese, who had been sent to weed the garden, with the words: 'Why, this child has absolutely nothing to do! What kind of a novice is she, if she must be sent for a walk every day?'

Therese, under the Rule that bound every moment of a nun's life, could make no reply. But she did more—she tried to accept such unjust reproaches and offer them up, like prayers, for the great causes she had in mind. She thought about her Christmas miracle, which seemed a long time ago now, and remembered how she had seen that every life, however simple, offered the opportunity for heroic sacrifices.

She had so little experience of the grown-up world, she turned back to the homely things of childhood as she tried to express her total readiness to put herself at the disposal of God.

'I imagined I was offering myself up to the Child Jesus like a toy, for him to do what he liked with me. I don't mean an expensive toy; give a child an expensive toy and he will sit looking at it without daring to touch it. But a toy of no value—a ball, say, is at his disposal; he can throw it on the ground, kick it about, make a hole in it, leave it lying in a corner, or press it to his heart if he feels that way about it. In the same way, I wanted Our Lord to do exactly what he liked with me.'

It fitted entirely into ideas like these, that her name 'in religion' was to be Therese of the Child Jesus, as she had hoped.

The difficult days of life as a postulant continued, while she tried to see each difficult moment as training for her life's work. At last, after nine months, she came to the day called her 'clothing,' when she would ceremonially put on the habit of a Carmelite.

# 6. The bride of Christ

IT WAS JUST eight days after her sixteenth birthday, January the 10th, 1889. By tradition it is always a great occasion, with the young Sister dressed as a bride, led to the altar by her father as she offers herself and her whole life to God.

M Martin wanted everything to be as fine as possible. Therese wore a dress of white velvet with a fine lace veil over her hair, worn long for the last time. She carried a spray of lilies, and she seemed filled with a spirit of quiet, undisturbed happiness.

'If I had anything better to give to God, I would offer it,' declared her father as she took his arm to enter the chapel.

She was received by the Bishop—the one she had gone to see in Bayeux less than two years before. As she approached him, he began to sing the Te Deum. A priest reminded him respectfully that this was sung only when a nun took her final vows. The Bishop motioned him away and continued the Te Deum, as if he was aware that the entry of Therese Martin into Carmel was an occasion for special thanksgiving.

Therese knelt before the Bishop, who asked her what she wanted. She replied: the mercy of God, the poverty of the order and the companionship of the Sisters.

'Are you here willingly and of your own free will, intending to love and serve God?' he asked her firmly.

'Yes,' she replied, just as firmly, 'with the help of God and the prayers of the Sisters.'

The Bishop blessed every article of the habit she would wear, and finally Therese herself. Then the sisters led her away. Her lovely wedding dress was laid aside, and she was clothed in the habit of the order. Then her long fair hair was cut short, as a sign that she was cutting herself free from all worldly vanities and distractions.

Finally, the white veil of a novice was put on her head, and a wreath of flowers over it.

She turned to the choir and lay on a carpet bordered with flowers. The Sisters, lighted candles in their hands, sang:

*Come, Holy Ghost, our souls inspire,*
*And lighten with celestial fire;*
*Thou the anointing Spirit art,*
*Who dost thy sevenfold gifts impart.*

Meanwhile Therese lay covered with her white choir cloak. By this ceremony the life of Therese Martin in the world was over. The life of Sister Therese of the Child Jesus had just begun.

Therese, born on January the 2nd, was a winter baby. She had always loved snow, and it was a family tradition that snow always fell on her birthday. On this day, her birthday into a new life, she was delighted when snow fell.

'Nothing was wanting, not even snow. The first

thing I saw when I got into the cloister was my favourite statue of the Child Jesus, smiling at me among the flowers and candles, and immediately afterwards—snowflakes!'

At last she had reached her goal. Her dream of becoming a Sister in Carmel was fulfilled.

'My dream wasn't a dream after all! Was I beside myself with joy? No, that's the wrong expression for it. It was rather the calm restful feeling which comes when you see the lighthouse which is going to guide you to harbour. The beacon of love now shone bright before me—I could reflect its beams.'

# 7. Glimpses of a hidden life

S O HER HIDDEN life as a nun in Carmel began. Yet in strange and unexpected ways there are flashes of light by which we can glimpse her life during the next few years.

They began only a few days after her 'Clothing', when a priest authorised by the Bishop had to enter Carmel on official business. Curiously he had a camera with him, and he took two photographs of Therese in the convent cloister. In one of them, she wore her white choir cloak; in the second, she took it off and appeared in her habit and white veil, a novice on the brink of her new life.

Pauline sent the photographs to their father; but she warned Celine not to show them to anyone outside the family, since the idea of photographs of a Carmelite nun was so strange.

Probably they were the last things on earth to give M Martin pleasure, for he became very ill and mentally disturbed, just as in Therese's vision of him years before.

She tried to make even this sorrow a part of her inner life, offering up her father's suffering and the unhappiness of her sisters to God.

At her father's death, three years later, Celine felt free to follow her own call and join her three sisters in Carmel. She found them changed.

Therese had now taken her final and permanent vows. She wore the black veil of the professed Carmelite. At her profession, she had altered her name in religion. She was no longer just a toy for the Child Jesus; she was a means by which his suffering could be reflected. She took the symbol of his likeness at his Passion: now she herself was called Sister Therese of the Child Jesus and the Holy Face.

Celine was to become Sister Genevieve of the Holy Face.

There was another change at Carmel. Mother Marie de Gonzague had come to the end of her term as prioress, and Mother Agnès de Jesus— Pauline— now reigned in her stead. She took a number of unusual steps.

Celine had a camera. It was rare for any young lady in the 1890s to take photographs, though some did. But Pauline gave Celine permission to take her camera into Carmel, where such a thing was entirely unknown. Celine had always been considered the family artist, and over the next few years she took a series of pictures of life in Carmel. From these we know what Therese looked like, and what she was doing, during what would otherwise have been the hidden period of her life.

It was Pauline, too, who was so convinced of the value of Therese's struggle to achieve complete union with the will of God that she ordered her 'under obedience' to write down the story of her spiritual life against the background of her earthly life. That is how Therese lives today, though her book, *The Story of a Soul*.

Why did Pauline do these things? She had always
been aware of great spiritual qualities in her little
sister. Did she want to preserve and record them,
and give her a chance to develop them further? Did
she foresee that some day a wider public would be
eager to see what Therese had written and would
value the pictures?

Could it be that she even dared to hope the Carmel at Lisieux and the Martin family had produced
a saint?

Therese herself, who as a child had declared she
chose everything, once told a priest she would like
to become a saint and serve God like the great lead-
ers of the Carmelite order. He was horrified at her
presumption, and told her to moderate the boldness
of her ambition.

She could not see that this was too bold. Our
Lord himself said 'You are to be perfect' she re-
called. Surely this meant a striving towards saint-
hood, which might be rewarded?

She was more and more convinced that an 'ordinary' life could lead to God, perhaps more easily than
a life lived in high places. 'I see clearly, like a true
daughter of his Blessed Mother, that Almighty God
has done great things in me, and the greatest of all
is to make me conscious of my own littleness.'

Pauline gave her a great opportunity to think out
these ideas, and to share them with other people.
She appointed Therese mistress of novices, in
charge of the young nuns in Carmel. Therese was
only twenty herself, but perhaps this may have been
a help, as her own difficult early days were not far
behind her. She was very successful: firm and tact-
ful and kind, and dedicated to her novices.

'You ask me what is the way I follow, which I
would like to tell everyone about. It is the way of

spiritual childhood—of complete confidence and self-abandonment.

'I want to show that there is only one thing necessary here on earth—to offer Jesus the gift of small sacrifices, and the oblation of loving acts. That is all I have been able to do, and only think how I have been rewarded.'

All the sisters, even the fully professed Carmelites, took their share of the household tasks. One day, while Therese was hard at work helping with the washing, another great opportunity was put before her. She would have thought it was very suitable that it should come at that time!

Mother Agnes of Jesus called her and told her she had just received a letter. It came from a young priest who was soon to go overseas as a missionary. He wanted to feel that back in France a nun would be praying constantly for him and his work. He begged that she would devote herself to the cause of his salvation and help him by her prayers and sacrifices, so that he would be the means of saving other souls.

Mother Agnes told Therese she wanted her to be a sister to the missionary in the making. Did the two sisters for a moment remember their parents and how they had longed for a little priest, perhaps even a missionary priest?

Therese was overjoyed at this new responsibility. 'It was such a strange fulfilment of my wish! Now, how can I cease to pray for all missionaries everywhere?'

Later other missionary priests were offered for her prayers, and she was allowed to write letters to them.

A new Carmelite convent was to be founded in Hanoi, in what was then French Indo-China.

Therese longed to be one of the sisters chosen to go there; but it was not to be. Yet because of her links with the missionary priests, her spiritual brothers, and the comfort her prayers have brought to those who followed them, she has a special place in the mission field.

In 1927 Pope Pius XI appointed her a patron of all foreign missions, alongside St Francis Xavier. He was a great missionary priest, four centuries ago, who travelled throughout the Far East and made many converts; while Therese barely left Normandy in France. Yet many missionaries, especially French priests, persecuted in Indo-China and hiding in the jungles of Laos, of Vietnam and Campuchea, find Therese a help and a consolation.

Therese herself was deeply grateful for her novices and her missionary priests. She thought of them as precious offerings she could make to God.

She prayed: 'Your love, Jesus, is an ocean with no shore to limit it, and if I plunge into it I carry with me all the possessions I have. You know, Lord, what these possessions are—the souls you have seen fit to link with mine—nothing else.'

# 8. *The end of the beginning*

THE YEARS progressed slowly. Pauline's three years as prioress came to an end, and Mother Marie de Gonzague was reappointed.

In spite of her dream of going to Hanoi, when Therese entered the Carmel at Lisieux she did not expect to leave it till her death. She believed—she would have said she knew—that after she died she would go to Heaven to be united for ever with God. The years between were only a time of waiting. So in every sense she looked forward to death. She was in Carmel for her earthly life.

Now, when she was twenty-three years old, she had a sign that her earthly life might not be long.

On Good Friday in 1896 she went to bed after keeping watch in the chapel. After she had put out her lantern she felt a strange liquid bubble up in her mouth. She did not feel ill or afraid, but in the morning, as it grew light, she saw her handkerchief was drenched with blood.

'My soul was flooded with joy at the thought that I was going to die,' she said.

As the Rule laid down, she told the Prioress; but her only concern was to carry on with the Holy

Week ritual. She shared not only in the services, but in the tremendous spring-cleaning before Easter. On the next day one of her novices saw her cleaning windows, looking desperately ill.

The haemorrhage following years of constant cold, shortage of sleep and little food meant that her health was fading fast, and she knew it. 'I shall die soon. I don't say it will be within a few months, but within two or three years at most.'

Her only wish was to continue to live in her cell and follow out the Rule, right to the end. 'God does not give one desires incapable of fulfilment,' she declared.

She struggled heroically. Her Sisters watched her climb the stairs, pausing painfully on each step before she could go on. It seemed such a short time since she had been a little girl climbing the stairs at Alencon, calling 'Maman! Maman!' on each step.

By winter she was so much weaker, she had to leave her cell, which saddened her greatly, and go to the convent infirmary. Doctors were allowed to attend her, but her illness was tuberculosis; and in those days there was no cure for it. The doctors tried various remedies, some painful, and none of them any good. She accepted them all patiently, knowing it was no use.

'Don't imagine, dear Mother, that your child is in a hurry to leave you,' she murmured to Pauline. 'I care for nothing, I want nothing except to do what Jesus wants. It's only that I can't help feeling glad when he seems to come so close, as if he were beckoning me to the glory of his kingdom.'

She lingered on, and when the summer came her illness seemed to withdraw a little. They got her a wheelchair, and she was able to sit out of doors under the chestnut trees. Whenever she was well enough, she worked on her writing. It had become very important to her that she should finish this before she died.

Often, though, other Sisters came up to her to say a friendly word, and interrupted her work. Mother Agnes tried to prevent this—she too thought the book was important—but Therese stopped her.

'I am supposed to be writing about brotherly love. This is one way I can show I believe in it.'

All too soon, the brief pause was over. She could no longer leave her bed in the infirmary. She was very weak and in great pain, often scarcely able to breathe.

Her real sisters were allowed to be with her con-

stantly. Only once did they hear her complain of
any of the hardships she had endured for the last
nine years.

'The thing that has troubled me most in my religious life has been the cold. Sometimes I have
thought I would die of it.'

Just as she had accepted those hardships, she
tried to accept her present illness as something she
could offer to God. 'It is very easy to write beautiful
things about suffering, but writing is nothing—
nothing at all. One must be in it to know. I wanted
to suffer a great deal for God, and truly I still want
to.'

One day, through her open window, she heard
one nun talking to another.

'Well,' she said, 'it seems that Sister Therese of
the Child Jesus is going to die before long. I can't
help wondering what the Prioress will find to say
about her afterwards. Really, I'm afraid she'll be
embarrassed! Because, after all, Sister Therese is
very nice, and all that, but she's never done anything worth talking about!'

Sometimes she thought so too, and was filled with
anguish that her life had been so useless, and that
she had made no kind of offering that God would
wish to accept. Had it all been for nothing? She
turned restlessly on her pillow.

'Oh, how one ought to pray for the dying! If only
people knew!'

Yet she struggled to make a sacrifice of her suffering, to offer it like prayer to bring other souls to
God.

Her sister asked her: 'You are in great pain just
now, aren't you?' and she replied: 'Yes, but I have
so longed for it!'

At last the fear that her life had been worthless

left her, and she was filled with radiant hope. As the end drew near, she was more and more convinced that all would be well. She began to speak with a new authority.

'You will look down on us from Heaven won't you, Sister Therese?' they asked her.

'No, I shall come down!'

As her Sisters nursed her devotedly, she thanked them with the words! 'You know, you are nursing a little saint!'

She saw ahead, far beyond her deathbed: 'I feel that my mission is just about to begin; the mission to make God loved as I love him myself, to show my own small way to small souls.'

Mother Agnes spoke of her idea that it might be possible to have Therese's writing published as a book. She found Therese was prepared for it.

'Everyone will see that it all comes from God, and whatever fame I may have will be a free gift which will not belong to me.'

Her Sisters bent over her to catch her last broken messages:

'You will not be unhappy after my death. I shall send you a rain of roses. . .

'I feel that all the world is going to love me. . .

'I shall spend my Heaven doing good upon earth. . .

Her sufferings in her last hours were agonising; her Sisters prayed for them to end.

One day Celine was sitting beside her when a dove flew in and perched by the open window. She smiled a little. It was her last moment of earthly pleasure, and her last day on earth.

That evening, as she held her crucifix, she breathed: 'I do not regret having given myself up to love. I love him—my God, I love you.' And then she breathed no more.

# 9. *A hurricane of glory*

S HE WAS BURIED quietly in the graveyard at Carmel, with a wooden cross over her grave. It said:

*Sister Therese of the Child Jesus*
*1873–1897*

Not long afterwards, her own words were added:

*I shall spend my heaven doing good upon earth.*

That might have been the end—the end of a pure and devout nun who had died young. But much more was to follow.

Her book was printed, and sent from Lisieux to every Carmelite convent in the world to tell them about their departed Sister. It was read eagerly, and greatly appreciated. Families and privileged friends were allowed to borrow it. Soon the book was published and read all over France; then in translation by Christians everywhere.

Because she seemed so young and so approachable, more and more people were drawn towards the Little Flower, and her Little Way towards God.

Before long prayers were being offered to Sister Therese of the Child Jesus, and often these prayers were answered.

'She is called, and she comes,' people said about her.

She seemed to be keeping her promise to send down a rain of roses in answered prayers and blessings.

A growing cry was heard that the Church should honour the Sister who could draw souls to God in this way, by making her a saint. Usually that takes centuries. The Church proceeds very slowly, setting up a judicial tribunal to weigh all the evidence, read every word, hear statements from hundreds of witnesses. There is a great unwillingness to make saints too easily.

St Joan, the other French girl who was made a saint, was not canonised until 500 years after her death.

The canonisation of Therese of Lisieux rushed forward, it was said, on 'a hurricane of glory'.

In 1910 the Bishop of Bayeux—the successor to Therese's old friend—was ordered to make a thorough investigation into the life and the writings of Therese, examining the life and virtues of the Servant of God.

Most of the people who had known Therese in her brief life were still alive—family, friends, sisters in Carmel. Pauline was ready to tell him every detail of her sister's story.

The evidence of her special qualities was so strong that the Pope ordered the process to start which would end in her being declared Blessed.

It was interrupted by the First World War. But devotions to Therese were increased in those years.

Mothers, wives, children, prayed for their loved ones; soldiers prayed to be kept safe in danger.

After the war, work began again. On May the 17th, 1925, less than thirty years after her death, a congregation of 60,000 people gathered in St Peter's in Rome, where Therese Martin had once begged to be allowed to become a Carmelite.

Half a million pilgrims gathered in the square outside. They heard the Pope, Piux XI, proclaim the heroic virtues of the new saint—Therese of the Child Jesus, the Little Flower of Lisieux.

All the power and the glory of the Catholic Church gathered in St Peter's to honour her, and that night the great dome was lit up with thousands and thousands of candles.

So many people wanted to go to Lisieux that work was started on an enormous church—a basilica overlooking the town—in honour of the town's own saint.

Then again war struck France. Lisieux was only thirty miles from the landing beaches of Normandy, where the allies swarmed in to liberate France, in the summer of 1944. Lisieux became a battlefield, with bombing raids over the town by British and American planes, and Germans setting fire to all the buildings that were left. The town became a buring furnace.

Carmel itself was right in the path of the flames. The sisters were told that they were in dreadful danger, and they were persuaded to leave Carmel. Led by Mother Agnes, who had been made Prioress in perpetuity, they left Carmel and sought sanctuary in the basilica overlooking the town.

From there they could see Lisieux ablaze, and Carmel likely to crumble in the fire. 'Oh, Saint Therese, save Carmel,' they begged.

By a miracle—or by the prayers of St Therese—Carmel was spared, as the fire died down. So too was Les Buissonnets, and the basilica itself.

Mother Agnes was able to take her nuns home. She died there herself in 1951 at a great age.

So it is possible to go to Lisieux today and walk in the footsteps of Saint Therese. And if pilgrims should pause for a moment to consider how strange it is that the Little Flower of Lisieux has become so widely known and loved, and so highly honoured by the Church, they must remember Therese's own words:

*Sanctity is not such and such a practice. It consists in a disposition of the heart, which renders us humble and pliant in the hands of God, conscious of our own weakness, but confident to the point of boldness in the goodness of our Heavenly Father.*